Oliver Herford

The Bashful Earthquake & other Fables and Verses

Oliver Herford

The Bashful Earthquake & other Fables and Verses

ISBN/EAN: 9783743318007

Manufactured in Europe, USA, Canada, Australia, Japa

Cover: Foto ©Thomas Meinert / pixelio.de

Manufactured and distributed by brebook publishing software (www.brebook.com)

Oliver Herford

The Bashful Earthquake & other Fables and Verses

The Bashful Earthquake

& *Other* FABLES
and VERSES by
OLIVER HERFORD
with many pictures
by *the Author*

New York: Published by
Charles Scribner's Sons in
the Autumn of MDCCCXCVIII

Copyright, 1898,
BY OLIVER HERFORD.

𝔘niversity 𝔓ress :
JOHN WILSON AND SON, CAMBRIDGE, U.S.A.

TO THE ILLUSTRATOR

IN GRATEFUL ACKNOWLEDGMENT OF HIS AMIABLE CONDESCENSION IN LENDING HIS EXQUISITELY DELICATE ART TO THE EMBELLISHMENT OF THESE POOR VERSES FROM HIS SINCEREST ADMIRER

THE AUTHOR

CONTENTS.

	PAGE
THE BASHFUL EARTHQUAKE	1
THE LOVESICK SCARECROW	7
THE MUSIC OF THE FUTURE	9
SONG	11
THE DOORLESS WOLF	12
THE BOLD BAD BUTTERFLY	15
CRUMBS	20
JAPANESQUE	21
THE DIFFERENCE	22
WHY YE BLOSSOME COMETH BEFORE YE LEAFE	23
THE FIRST FIRST OF APRIL	24
THE EPIGRAMMATIST	26
THE SILVER LINING	28
THE BOASTFUL BUTTERFLY	31
THE THREE WISHES	35
TRUTH	37
THE TRAGIC MICE	38
ABSENCE OF MIND	40
THE GRADUATE	41
THE POET'S PROPOSAL	44
A THREE-SIDED QUESTION	45
THE SNAIL'S DREAM	51

	PAGE
A Christmas Legend	52
Hyde and Seeke	54
In the Café	55
The Legend of the Lily	58
The Untutored Giraffe	60
The Enchanted Wood	64
A Bunny Romance	68
The Flower Circus	72
The Fatuous Flower	77
A Love Story	80
Ye Knyghte-Mare	83
Metaphysics	84
The Princess that wasn't	86
The Lion's Tour	89
The Fugitive Thought	93
The Cussed Damozel	97
A Gas-log Reverie	101
Cupid's Fault	103
All Aboard	104
Killing Time	105
The Mermaid Club	107
A Song	109
Angel's Toys	110
The Reformed Tigress	112
Two Ladies	115
To the Wolf at the Door	119
The Fall of J. W. Beane	121

CRIME, Wickedness, Villany, Vice, -
 And Sin only misery bring;
If you want to be Happy and Nice,
 Be good and all that sort of thing.

The Bashful Earthquake

THE Earthquake rumbled
And mumbled
   And grumbled;
And then he bumped,
And everything tumbled —
   Bumpyty-thump!
   Thumpyty-bump! —
Houses and palaces all in a lump!

"Oh, what a crash!
Oh, what a smash!
How could I ever be so rash?"
The Earthquake cried.
"What under the sun
Have I gone and done?
I never before was so mortified!"
Then away he fled,
And groaned as he sped:
"This comes of not looking before I tread."

Out of the city along the road
He staggered, as under a heavy load,
Growing more weary with every league,
Till almost ready to faint with fatigue.
He came at last to a country lane
Bordering upon a field of grain;
And just at the spot where he paused to rest,
In a clump of wheat, hung a Dormouse nest.

The sun in the west was sinking red,
And the Dormouse had just turned into bed,

Dreaming as only a Dormouse can,
When all of a sudden his nest began
To quiver and shiver and tremble and shake.
Something was wrong, and no mistake!

In a minute the Dormouse was wide awake,
And, putting his head outside his nest,
Cried: "WHO IS IT DARES DISTURB MY REST?"

His voice with rage was a husky squeak.
The Earthquake by now had become so weak
He'd scarcely strength enough to speak.
He even forgot
the rules of
grammar;
All he could
do was to
feebly stammer:

"I'm sorry, but I'm afraid it's me.
Please don't be angry. I'll try to be —"

No one will know what he meant to say,
For all at once he melted away.

. . . .

The Dormouse, grumbling, went back to bed,
"Oh, bother the Bats!" was all he said.

The Lovesick Scarecrow

A SCARECROW in a field of corn,
A thing of tatters all forlorn,
Once felt the influence of Spring
And fell in love — a foolish thing,
And most particularly so
In his case — *for he loved a crow!*

"Alack-a-day! it's wrong, I know,
It's wrong for me to love a crow;
An all-wise man created me
To scare the crows away," cried he;
"And though the music of her 'Caw'
Thrills through and through this heart of straw,

"My passion I must put away
And do my duty, come what may!
Yet oh, the cruelty of fate!
I fear she doth reciprocate
My love, for oft at dusk I hear
Her in my cornfield hovering near.

"And once I dreamt — oh, vision blest!
That she alighted on my breast.
'T is very, very hard, I know,
But all-wise man decreed it so."
He cried and flung his arm in air,
The very picture of despair.

. . . . . .

Poor Scarecrow, if he could but know!
Even now his lady-love, the Crow,
Sits in a branch, just out of sight,
With her good husband, waiting night,
To pluck from out his sleeping breast
His heart of straw to line her nest.

THE politest musician that ever was seen
Was Montague Meyerbeer Mendelssohn Green.
So extremely polite he would take off his hat
Whenever he happened to meet with a cat.

"It's not that I'm partial to cats," he'd explain;
"Their music to me is unspeakable pain.
There's nothing that causes my flesh so to crawl
As when they perform a G-flat caterwaul.

Yet I cannot help feeling — in spite of their din —
When I hear at a concert the first violin
Interpret some exquisite thing of my own,
If it were not for *cat gut* I'd never be known.

And so, when I bow as you see to a cat,
It is n't to *her* that I take off my hat;
But to fugues and sonatas that possibly hide
Uncomposed in her — well — in her tuneful inside!"

SONG.

Gather Kittens while you may,
  Time brings only Sorrow;
And the Kittens of To-day
  Will be Old Cats To-morrow.

THE DOORLESS WOLF.

I saw, one day, when times were very good,
A newly rich man walking in a wood,
Who chanced to meet, all hungry, lean, and sore,
The wolf that used to sit outside his door.
Forlorn he was, and piteous his plaint.
"Help me!" he howled. "With hunger I am faint.
It is so long since I have seen a door —
And you are rich, and you have many score.
When you'd but one, I sat by it all day;
Now you have many, I am turned away.
Help me, good sir, once more to find a place.
Prosperity now stares me in the face."

The newly rich man, jingling all the while
The silver in his pocket, smiled a smile:
He saw a way the wolf could be of use.
"Good wolf," said he, "you're going to the deuce, —
The dogs, I mean, — and that will never do;
I think I've found a way to see you through.
I too have worries. Ever since I met
Prosperity I have been sore beset

By begging letters, charities, and cranks,
All very short in gold and long in thanks.
Now, if you'll come and sit by my front door
From eight o'clock each morning, say, till four,

Then every one will think that I am poor,
And from their pesterings I'll be secure.
Do you accept?" The wolf exclaimed, "I do!"
The rich man smiled; the wolf smiled; *I* smiled, too,
And in my little book made haste to scrawl:
"Thus affluence makes niggards of us all!"

The Bold Bad Butterfly

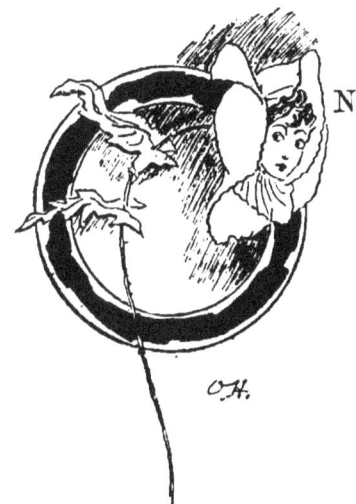

ONE day a Poppy, just in play,
   Said to a butterfly, " Go 'way,
   Go 'way, you naughty thing! Oh, my!
   But you 're a bold bad butterfly!"

Of course 't was only said in fun,
   He was a perfect paragon —
   In every way a spotless thing
   (Save for two spots upon his wing).

But tho' his morals were the best,
He could not understand a jest;
And somehow what the Poppy said
Put ideas in his little head,
And soon he really came to wish
He *were* the least bit " devilish."

He then affected manners rough
And strained his voice to make it gruff,
And scowled as who should say "Beware,
I am a dangerous character.
You'd best not fool with me, for I —
I am a bold, bad butterfly."

He hung around the wildest flowers,
And kept the most unseemly hours,
With dragonflies and drunken bees,
And learned to say "By Jove!" with ease,
Until his pious friends, aghast,
Exclaimed, "He's getting awf'lly fast!"

He shunned the nicer flowers, and threw
Out hints of shady things he knew
About the laurels, and one day
He even went so far to say
Something about the lilies sweet
I could not possibly repeat!

At length, it seems, from being told
How bad he was, he grew so bold,
This most obnoxious butterfly,
That one day, swaggering 'round the sky,
He swaggered in the net of Mister Jones, the entomologist.

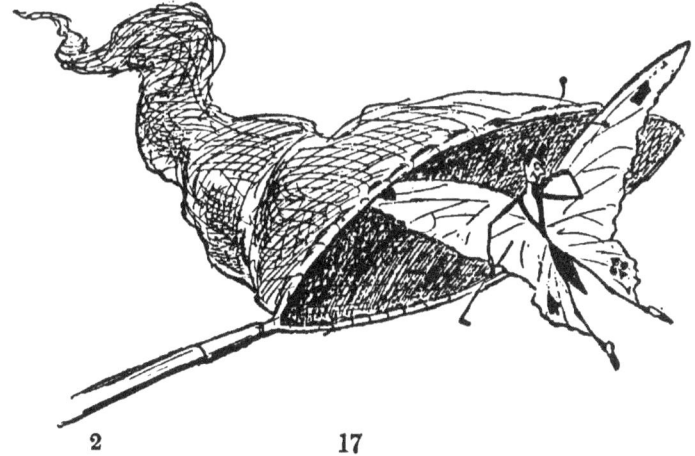

"It seems a sin," said Mr. J.,
"This harmless little thing to slay,"
As, taking it from out his net,
He pinned it to a board, and set
Upon a card below the same,
In letters large, its Latin name,
Which is —

but I omit it, lest
Its family might be distressed,
And stop the little sum per year
They pay me not to print it here.

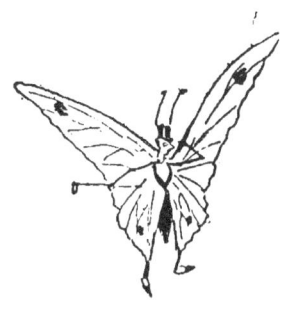

CRUMBS.

UP to my frozen window-shelf
    Each day a begging birdie comes,
And when I have a crust myself
    The birdie always gets the crumbs.

    They say who on the water throws
His bread, will get it back again;
    If that is true, perhaps — who knows? —
I have not cast my crumbs in vain.

Indeed, I know it is not quite
    The thing to boast of one's good deed;
To what the left hand does, the right,
    I am aware, should pay no heed.

Yet if in modest verse I tell
    My tale, some editor, maybe,
May like it very much, and — well,
    My bread will then return to me.

Japanesque

OH, where the white quince blossom swings
    I love to take my Japan ease!
I love the maid Anise who clings
    So lightly on my Japan knees;
I love the little song she sings,
    The little love-song Japanese.
I *almost* love the lute's *tink tunkle*
    Played by that charming Jap
        Anise —
For am I not her old Jap uncle?
    And is she not my Japan
        niece?

THE DIFFERENCE.

IN the spring the Leaves come out
And the little Poetlets sprout;
Everywhere they may be seen,
Each as Fresh as each is Green.
Each hangs on through scorch and scoff
Till the fall, when both "come off,"
With this difference, be it said,
That the leaves at least are Red.

WHY YE BLOSSOME COMETH BEFORE YE LEAFE.

ONCE hoary Winter chanced — alas!
Alas! hys waye mistaking,
A leafless apple tree to pass
Where Spring lay dreaming. "Fie ye lass!
Ye lass had best be waking,"
Quoth he, and shook hys robe, and lo!
Lo! forth didde flye a cloud of snowe.

Now in ye bough an elfe there dwelte,
An elfe of wondrous powere,
That when ye chillye snowe didde pelte,
With magic charm each flake didde melte,
Didde melte into a flowere;
And Spring didde wake and marvelle how,
How blossomed so ye leafless bough.

The First First of April.

The Infant Earth one April day
(The first of April — so they say),
When toddling on her usual round,
Spied in her path upon the ground
A dainty little garland ring
Of violets — and *that* was Spring.
She caught the pretty wreath of Spring
And all the birds began to sing,
But when she thought to hold it tight
'T was rudely jerked from out her sight;
And while she looked for it in vain
The birds all flew away again.

Alas! The flowering wreath of Spring
Was fastened to a silken string,
And Time, the urchin, laughed for glee
(He held the other end you see).

And that was long ago, they say,
When Time was young and Earth was gay.
Now Earth is old and Time is lame,
Yet still they play the same old game :
Old Earth still reaches out for Spring,
And Time — well — Time still holds the string.

THE EPIGRAMMATIST.

I KNOW an entomologist
   Who thinks it not a sin
To catch a harmless butterfly,
   And stick it, with a pin,
Upon a piece of paper white,
   And underneath the same,
In letters large and plain, to write
   The creature's Latin name.

I know another little man
   Who catches, now and then,
A microscopic little thought
   And goads it, with a pen,
To rhyme, until we wonder quite
   How it can keep so tame,
And why he never fails to write
   Beneath (in *full*) his name.

If you should ask me to decide
　　The which of them I'd rate
The greater torment of the two
　　I should not hesitate.
It's wicked with a pin to bore
　　A butterfly — but then,
I loathe the other fellow more,
　　Who bores me with his pen.

THE SILVER LINING.

WHEN poets sing of lovers' woes,
    And blighted lives and throbs and throes
And yearnings — goodness only knows
    It's all a pose.

I am a poet too, you know,
    I too was young once long ago,
And wrote such stuff myself, and so
    I ought to know.

I too found refuge from Despair
 In sonnets to Amanda's fair
White brow or Nell's complexion rare
 Or Titian hair —

Which, when she scorned, did I resign
 To flames, and go into decline?
Not much! When sonnets fetched per line
 Enough to dine.

So, reader, when you read in print
 A poet's woe — beware and stint
Your tears — and take this gentle hint
 It is his mint.

When Julia's *"fair as flowery mead,"*
  Or when she *"makes his heart-strings bleed,"*
Know then she's furnishing his feed
  Or fragrant weed —

And even as you read — who knows?
  Like cannibal that eats his foes,
He dines off Julia's *"heart that froze,"*
  Or *"cheek of Rose."*

THE BOASTFUL BUTTERFLY.

(FROM THE ORIENTAL.)

Upon the temple dome
  Of Solomon the wise
There paused, returning home,
  A pair of butterflies.

He did the quite blasé
  (Did it rather badly),
Wherefore — need I say? —
  She adored him madly.

Enthusiasm she
   Did not attempt to curb:
"Goodness gracious me!
   Is n't this superb!"

He vouchsafed a smile
   To indulge her whimsy,
Surveyed the lofty pile,
   And drawled, "Not bad — but flimsy!

"Appearances, though fine,
   Lead to false deduction;
This temple, I opine,
   Is shaky in construction.

"Think of it, my dear.
   All this glittering show
Would crumble — disappear —
   Should I but stamp my toe!

"If I should stamp — like this —"
   His wife cried, "Heavens! *don't!*"
He answered, with a kiss,
   "Very well; I won't."

Now, every blessed word
   Said by these butterflies,
It chanced, was overheard
   By Solomon the wise.

He called in angry tone,
   And bade a Djinn to hie
And summon to his throne
   That boastful butterfly.

The butterfly flew down
   Upon reluctant wing.
Cried Solomon, with a frown,
   "How dared you
     say this thing?

"How dared you,
   fly, invent
Such blasphemy
   as this is?"

"Oh, king, I only meant
 To terrify the missis."

The insect was so scared
 The king could scarce restrain
A smile. "Begone! you're spared;
 But don't do it again!"

So spake King Solomon.
 The *butterflew* away.
His wife to meet him ran:
 "Oh, dear, what *did* he say?"

The butterfly had here
 A chance to shine, and knew it.
Said he: "The king, my dear,
 Implored me *not to do it!*"

The Three Wishes.

ONCE to a man a goblin came
 And said to him, "If you will name
 Three wishes, whatsoe'er they be,
 They shall be granted instantly.
 Think of three things you deem the best,
Express your wish — '*we do the rest.*' "
"O Goblin!" cried the man, "indeed
You 're just the kind of a friend I need.
Hunger and Want I 've known thus far,
I fain would learn what Riches are."
"Then," cried the Goblin, "learn it well,
Riches are title deeds to Hell!
Now wish again."

"Alackaday!"
Exclaimed the man. "I've thrown away,
And all for naught, a chance immense;
I only wish I had some sense!"
The Goblin waved his hand — the Dunce
To his surprise was wise for once.
And being wise, he laughed, and said:
"I am a fool — would I were dead!"
. . . .
"Granted!" the Goblin yell'd "it's plain
You'll never be so wise again."

TRUTH.

PERMIT me, madame, to declare
That I never will compare
Eyes of yours to Starlight cold,
Or your locks to Sunlight's gold,
Or your lips, I 'd have you know,
To the crimson Jacqueminot.

Stuff like that 's all very fine
When you get so much a line;
Since I don't, I scorn to tell
Flattering lies. I like too well
Sun and Stars and Jacqueminot
To flatter them, I 'd have you know.

THE TRAGIC MICE.

It was a tragic little mouse
   All bent on suicide
Because another little mouse
   Refused to be his bride.

"Alas!" he squeaked, "I shall not wed!
   My heart and paw she spurns;
I'll hie me to the cat instead,
   From whence no mouse returns!"

The playful cat met him half way,
   Said she, "I feel for you,
You're dying for a mouse, you say,
   I'm dying for one, too!"

Now when Miss Mouse beheld his doom,
   Struck with remorse, she cried,
"In death we'll meet! — O cat! make room
   For one more mouse inside."

The playful cat was charmed; said she,
"I shall be, in a sense,
Your pussy catafalque!" Ah me!
It was her last offence!

. . . . .

Reader, take warning from this tale,
And shun the punster's trick:
*Those mice, for fear lest cats might fail,
Had eaten arsenic!*

ABSENCE OF MIND.

THEY paused just at the crossing's brink.
Said she, "We must turn back, I think."
She eyes the mud. He sees her shrink,
  Yet does not falter,
But recollects with fatal tact
That cloak upon his arm — in fact,
Resolves to do the courtly act
  Of good Sir Walter.

Why is it that she makes no sound,
Staring aghast as on the ground
He lays the cloak with bow profound?
  Her utterance chokes her.
She stands as petrified, until,
Her voice regained, in accents chill
She gasps, "*I'll thank you if you will
  Pick up my cloak, sir!*"

The Graduate.

"YOU are old," 'Father World,' cried
    the Graduate,
"But for one of your age and size,
I feel it is only my duty to state
    You *are* not uncommonly wise."

"I *am* aged," replied Father World, "it is true.
    And not very wise I agree.
Do you think tho' it's fair for a scholar like you
    To abuse an old fossil like me?"

Said the youth, "I refer not to college degrees,
    Nor dates that one crams in his skull,
I complain not because you are lacking in these,
    But because you're so awfully dull!

"I have studied you now I should think more or less
   For twenty-one years, and I know
You right through and through, and I can but confess
   You are really confoundedly slow."

Said the world, "My dear sir, you are right, there's no crime
   Like dulness — henceforth I will try
To be clever — forgive me! I'm taking your time,
   Perhaps we'll meet later! Good-bye!"

LATER.

"You are cold, Father World, and harden'd forsooth,"
  Cried the man, "and exceeding wise,
And for any offensive remarks of my youth
  I beg to apologize."

THE POET'S PROPOSAL.

"PHYLLIS, if I could I 'd paint you
As I see you sitting there,
　You distracting little saint, you,
With your aureole of hair.
　If I only *were* an artist,
And such glances could be caught,
　You should have the very smartest
Picture frame that can be bought!

"Phyllis, since I can't depict your
Charms, or give you aught but fame,
　Will you be yourself the picture?
Will you let me be the frame?
　Whose protecting clasp may bind you
Always—"

　"Nay," cried Phyllis; "hold,
Or you 'll force me to remind you
　Paintings *must* be framed with gold!"

A Three-sided Question

Scene. A hollow tree in the woods.
Time. December evening.

    Mr. Owl.
    Mr. Sparrow.
    Mr. Bear.

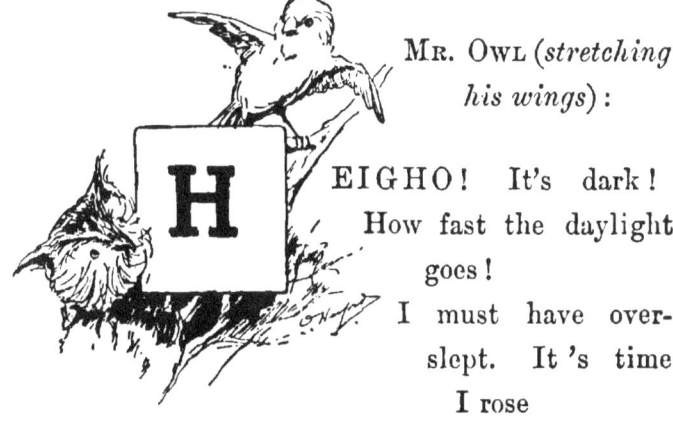

Mr. Owl (*stretching his wings*):

HEIGHO! It's dark!
How fast the daylight goes!
I must have overslept. It's time I rose
And went about my breakfast to prepare.
I should keep better hours; I declare,

Before I got to bed 't was broad daylight!
That must be why I'm getting up to-night
With such a sleepy feeling in my head.
Heigho! Heigho! (*Yawns.*)

Enter MR. SPARROW.

MR. SPARROW: Why don't you go to bed,
If you're so very sleepy? — it's high time!
The sun has set an hour ago, and I'm
Going home myself as fast as I can trot.
Night is the time for sleep.
   MR. OWL: The time for *what*?
The time for *sleep*, you say?
   MR. SPARROW: That's what I said.
   MR. OWL:
Well, my dear bird, your reason must have fled!

Mr. Sparrow (*icily*):
I do not catch your meaning quite, I fear.
Mr. Owl:
I mean you're talking nonsense. Is that clear?
Mr. Sparrow (*angrily*):
Say that again — again, sir, if you dare!
Say it again!
Mr. Owl: As often as you care.
You're talking nonsense — stuff and nonsense —
 there!
Mr. Sparrow (*hopping one twig higher up*):
You are a coward, sir, and *impolite!*
 (*Hopping on a still higher twig*)
And if you were n't beneath me I would fight.
Mr. Owl:
I *am* beneath you, true enough, my friend,
By just two branches. Will you not descend?
Or shall I —
Mr. Sparrow (*hastily*):
 No, don't rise. Tell me instead
What was the nonsense that you thought I said.
Mr. Owl:
It may be wrong, but if I heard aright,
You said the proper time for sleep was night.
Mr. Sparrow:
That's what I said, and I repeat it too!

MR. OWL:
Then you repeat a thing that is not true.
Day is the time for sleep, not *night*.

MR. SPARROW: Absurd!
Who's talking nonsense now?

MR. OWL: Impudent bird!
How dare you answer back, you upstart fowl!

MR. SPARROW: How dare you call me upstart — you — you — *Owl!*

MR. OWL: This is too much! I'll stand no more, I vow! Defend yourself!

Mr. Bear (*looking out of hollow tree*) :
Come, neighbors, stop that row!
What you 're about I 'm sure I cannot think.
I only know I have n't had one wink
Of sleep.   Indeed, I 've borne it long enough.
'T would put the mildest temper in a huff;

And I am but a bear.   Why don't you go
To bed like other folks, I 'd like to know?

Summer is long enough to keep awake —
Winter's the time when honest people take
Their three months' sleep.

   Mr. Sparrow: That settles me! I fly!
Dear Mr. Owl and Mr. Bear, good-by!   [*Exit.*
  Mr. Owl:
I must go too, to find another wood.
Every one's mad in this queer neighborhood!
It is not safe such company to keep.
Good evening, Mr. Bear.   [*Exit.*
  Mr. Bear: *Now* I shall sleep.

CURTAIN.

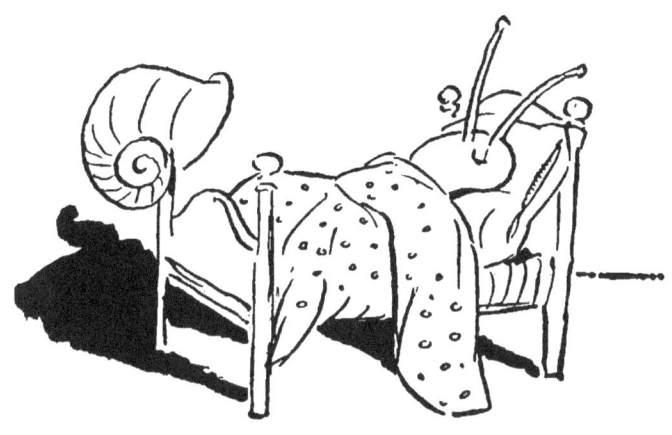

THE SNAIL'S DREAM.

A SNAIL, who had a way, it seems,
Of dreaming very curious dreams,
Once dreamed he was — you'll never guess ! —
The Lightning Limited Express !

A CHRISTMAS LEGEND.

BENEATHE an ancient oake one daye
A holye friar kneeled to praye;
Scarce hadde he mumbled Aves three,
When lo! a voice within the tree!
Straighte to the friar's hearte it wente,
A voice as of some spirit pente
Within the hollow of the tree,
That cried, "Good father, sette me free!"

Quoth he, "This hath an evil sounde."
Ande bente him lower to the grounde.
But ever tho' he prayed, the more
The voice hys pytie didde implore,
Untyl he raised hys eyes ande there
Behelde a mayden ghostlie faire.
Thus to the holy manne she spoke:

"*Within the hollow of this oak,*
Enchanted for a hundred yeares,
Have I been bounde — yet vain my teares;
Notte anything can breake the banne
Till I be kiss'd by holye manne."

"Woe's me!" thenne sayd the friar; "if thou
Be sente to tempt me breake my vowe;
Butte whether mayde or fiende thou be,
I'll stake my soul to sette thee free."
The holye manne then crossed hym thrice,
And kissed the mayde — when in a trice
She vanished —
     "Heaven forgive me now!"
Exclaimed the friar — "my broken vowe.

"If I have sinned — I sinned to save
Another fromme a living grave."
Thenne downe upon the earth he felle,
And prayed some sign that he might telle
If he were doomed for-evermore;
When lo! the oake, alle bare before,
Put forth a branch of palest greene,
And fruited everywhere betweene
With waxen berries, pearlie white,
A miracle before hys sight.
 . . . . . .
The holye friar wente hys waye
And told hys tale —
     And from thatte daye
It hath been writ that anye manne
May blamelesse kiss what mayde he canne
Nor any one shall say hym "no"
Beneath the holye mistletoe.

HYDE AND SEEKE.

ONE day beneathe a willowe tree,
  Love met a mayde moste faire to see;
"Come play at hyde and seeke," cried he.
"With alle my hearte!" — quoth she.

"I 'm it!" Love cries, and rounde hys eyes
  A scarfe the maiden bindeth,
And inne and oute and rounde aboute
  Ye willowe trees he windeth —
  Yette ne'er the maiden findeth.

Stille inne and oute and rounde aboute,
  And stille no maiden meetinge;
Till, piqued, ye rogue unbinds hys eyes,
And, perched upon a branch, espies
  Ye mayde retreatinge;
"Fie! Fie!" cries Love — "you 're cheetinge!"

"Now, you," quothe he, "must seeke for me!"
  She binds her eyes, assentinge,
And inne and oute and rounde aboute,
  Seeks she for Love relentinge —

But Love, they say — alas, ye day!
Has spread his wings and flown away,
  And left ye mayde lamentinge,
  And left ye mayde repentinge.

IN THE CAFÉ.

1 P. M.

He sits before me as I write,
    And talks of this and that,
And all my thoughts are put to flight
    By his infernal chat.
I came to write a tender rhyme
    To Phyllis or to Mabel,
And chose in this retired café
    The most secluded table.
He came before I'd time to fly,
    And ere I could refuse,

         Had filled the very chair that I
            Was keeping for the muse!
         Then came the deluge — down it came
            In one unceasing pour —
         Of science, crops, photography,
            Religion, soups, and war.

1.30 — Forsooth the flood of words that flows
            From this secluded table
         Will soon be great enough to swamp
            A dozen towers of Babel.
2.30 — And still he stays, and still the flood
            Is rising as before;
3 —   The world is now a sea of words
3.30 — Without a sign of shore.
            .   .   .   .   .

6 —   Great Scott! He's going!
                     "No, *must* you go?
         Don't tear yourself away!
         What have I written? Oh, some trash —
            A sort of Fairy-lay,
         Of how a dreadful ogre
            Caught a luckless youth one day,
         And drowned him in a flood of — well,
            If you *must* go — *good* day!"

ENVOY.

Phyllis — or Mabel! pray forgive —
I had to pay him out;
I'll write that tender rhyme to you
Some other day, no doubt.

THE LEGEND OF THE LILY.

ONCE a Tiger for a freak,
  Fell in love
    With a Lily, pure and meek
And as timid, white, and weak
    As a dove.
Yet withal a wee bit chilly,
Just enough the Tiger's silly
    Pride to pique.

By and by the Lily cold,
    Felt the charm;
    Learned, tho' dreadful to behold,
That the Tiger, fierce and bold,
    Meant no harm.
And she smiled upon him shyly,
Till at length the Tiger wily
    Was consoled.

So in time the Beauty grew
    To adore
The Royal Beast who came to woo,
Loved him for his golden hue —
    For his roar;
All for him with blushes burning,
To a Tiger-lily turning,
    Golden too.

But alas, the luckless Lily
    Loved in vain;
For a painted daffodilly
Came between them, and the Lily,
    Pale with pain,
In a dark pool, drooped and pining,
Drowned herself, and rose a shining
    Water-lily.

The Untutored Giraffe.

A CHILD at school who fails to pass
Examination in his class
Of Natural History will be
So shaky in Zoölogy,
That, should he ever chance to go
To foreign parts, he scarce will know
The common *Mus Ridiculus*
From *Felis* or *Caniculus*.
And what of boys and girls is true
Applies to other creatures, too,
As you will cheerfully admit
When once I 've illustrated it.

Once on a time a young Giraffe
(Who when at school devoured the chaff,
And trampled underneath his feet
The golden grains of Learning's wheat)
Upon his travels chanced to see
A Python hanging from a tree,
A thing he 'd never met before.
All neck it seemed and nothing more ;
And, stranger still, it was bestrown
With pretty spots much like his own.
Well, well ! I 've often heard," he said,
" Of foolish folk who lose their head;
But really it 's a funnier joke
To meet a head that 's lost its folk.

" Dear me! Ha! ha! It makes me laugh.
Where *has* he left his other half ?
If he could find it he would be
A really fine Giraffe, like me."

The Python, waking with a hiss,
Exclaimed, "What kind of snake is this?
Your spots are really very fine,
Almost as good in fact as mine,
But with those legs I fail to see
How you can coil about a tree.
Take away half, and you would make
A very decent sort of snake —
Almost as fine a snake as I;
Indeed, it's not too late to try."

A something in the Python's eye
Told the Giraffe 't was best to fly,
Omitting all formality.
And afterward, when safe at home,
He wrote a very learned tome,
Called, "What I Saw beyond the Foam."
Said he, "The strangest thing one sees
Is a Giraffe who hangs from trees,

And has — (right here the author begs
To state a *fact*) and has *no legs!*"

The book made a tremendous hit.
The public all devoured it,
Save one, who, minding how he missed
Devouring the author — *hissed*.

The Enchanted Wood.

A DARK old Raven lived in a tree,
With a little Tree-frog for company,

In the midst of a forest so thick with trees
Only thin people could walk with ease.

Yet though the forest was dank and dark,
The little Tree-frog was gay as a lark;

He piped and trilled the livelong day,
While the Raven was just the other way:

He grumbled and croaked from morn till night,
And nothing in all the world was right.

The moon was too pale, or the sun too bright;
The sky was too blue, or the snow too white;

The thrushes too gay, or the owls too glum;
And the squirrels — well, they were too squirrelsome.

And as for the trees, *why* did they grow
In a wood, of all places? — he'd like to know.

A wood is so dark and unhealthy, too,
For trees; and besides, they obstruct the view.

And so it went on from morn till night:
The Tree-frog piping with pure delight,

And the Raven croaking with all his might
That nothing in all the world was right.

Well, in this same wood, it chanced one day
The enchanter Merlin lost his way;

And stopping to rest 'neath the very tree
Where the Raven and Tree-frog were taking their tea,

He divined of a sudden, by magic lore,
A thing I forgot to mention before :

That the forest and all that therein did dwell
Owed their present shape to an ancient spell.

Now a spell, though a tiresome job to make,
Is the easiest thing in the world to break,

When once you know how to perform the trick,
As Merlin did. Waving his magic stick,

He cried, "Let this forest and everything in it
Take its former shape!" When lo! in a minute,

In place of the Raven, a stern old sage
All robed in black and all bent with age;

And where the little Tree-frog had been
Sat a goodly youth all dressed in green;

And around about was a flowery lawn
Where the forest had been. Said the sage, with a
 yawn:

"I must have been dozing — well, to resume —
As I was saying, this world of gloom —"

"Oh, bother the world of gloom — just hear
That thrush!" cried the youth; "the first this
 year!"

A BUNNY ROMANCE.

THE Bunnies are a feeble folk
    Whose weakness is their strength.
    To shun a gun a Bun will run
    To almost any length.

    Now once, when war alarms were rife
  In the ancestral wood
Where the kingdom of the Bunnies
  For centuries had stood,
The king, for fear long peace had made
  His subjects over-bold,
To wake the glorious spirit
  Of timidity of old,

Announced one day he would bestow
    Princess Bunita's hand
On the Bunny who should prove himself
    Most timid in the land.

Next day a proclamation
    Was posted in the wood
"To the Flower of Timidity,
    The Pick of Bunnyhood:
His Majesty the Bunny king,
    Commands you to appear
At a tournament — at such a date
    In such and such a year —
Where his Majesty will then bestow
    Princess Bunita's hand
On the Bunny who will prove himself
    Most timid in the land."

Then every timid Bunny's heart
    Swelled with exultant fright
At the thought of doughty deeds of fear
    And prodigies of flight.

For the motto of the Bunnies
    As perhaps you are aware,
Is "Only the faint-hearted
    Are deserving of the fair."

They fell at once to practising,
    These Bunnies, one and all,
Till some could almost die of fright
    To hear a petal fall.
And one enterprising Bunny
    Got up a special class
To teach the art of fainting
    At your shadow on the grass.

At length — at length — at length
    The moment is at hand!
And trembling all from head to foot
    A hundred Bunnies stand.
And a hundred Bunny mothers
    With anxiety turn gray
Lest their offspring dear should lose their fear
    And linger in the fray.

Never before in Bunny lore
    Was such a stirring sight
As when the bugle sounded
    To begin the glorious flight!
A hundred Bunnies, like a flash,
    All disappeared from sight
Like arrows from a hundred bows —
    None swerved to left or right.
Some north, some south, some east, some west, —
    And none of them, 't is plain,
Till he has gone around the earth
    Will e'er be seen again.

It may be in a hundred weeks,
    Perchance a hundred years.
Whenever it may be, 't is plain
    The one who first appears
Is the one who ran the fastest;
    He wins the Princess' hand,
And gains the glorious title of
    " Most Timid in the Land."

THE FLOWER CIRCUS.

The flowers in the dell
   Once gave a circus show;
And as I know them well,
   They asked if I would go
As their especial guest.
" Quite charmed!" said I, and so
Put on my very best
   Frock-coat and shiny hat,

And my embroidered vest
  And wonderful cravat;
In fact, no end of style,
  For it is, as you know,
But once in a great while
  The flowers give a show.

They gave me a front seat,
  The very nicest there —
A bank of violets sweet
  And moss and maidenhair.
'T was going to be a treat —
  I felt it in the air.

As martial music crashed
  From a trained trumpet-vine,
Into the ring there dashed
  A beauteous columbine!
With airy grace she strode
  Her wild horse-chestnut steed.

I held my breath, she rode
  With such terrific speed.
They brought a cobweb ring,
  And lightly she jumped through it.
(A very dangerous thing;
  How *did* she learn to do it?)

I cried, "Brava! Encore!"
  Until she'd jumped through nine,
Each higher than before.
  (I tell you, it was fine!)

Then Jack-in-pulpit — who
  From out his lofty place
Announced what each would do —
  Cried, "Next there comes a race."

Two Scarlet Runners flew
  Three times the ring around,
And with a crown of dew
  The winner's head was crowned.

A booby race, for fun,
  Came next (the prize was cheaper).
Trailing Arbutus won
  Over Virginia Creeper.

Then came the world-famed six,
    The Johnny-jump-up Brothers,
Who did amazing tricks,
    Each funnier than the others.

A Spider, in mid-air
    (Engaged at great expense),
On tight-thread gossamer
    Danced with a skill immense!

A dashing young Green Blade
    Who quickly followed suit,
An exhibition made
    Of how young blades can shoot.

There were Harebell ringers, too,
    Who played delightful tunes,
And trained Dog-violets, who
    Did antics, like buffoons.
All these and more were there —
    Too many for narration;
But nothing could compare
    With the last " Great Sensation."

I never shall forget,
    Though I should live an age,
The sight of Mignonette
    Within the Lion's cage.
Sweet smiling Mignonette!
    Not one bit scared — for why on
Earth should she fear her pet,
    Her dear, tame Dandelion?

THE FATUOUS FLOWER.

ONCE on a time a Bumblebee Addressed a Sunflower. Said he: "Dear Sunflower, tell me is it true What everybody says of you?"

Replied the Sunflower: "Tell me, pray,
How should *I* know what people say?
Why should I even care? No doubt
'T is some ill-natured tale without
A word of truth; but tell me, Bee,
What *is* it people say of me?"
"Oh, no!" the Bee made haste to add;
"'T is really not so very bad.
I got it from the Ant. She said
She'd *heard* the Sun had turned your head,

And that whene'er he
walks the skies
You follow him with all
your eyes
From morn till eve—"
"Oh, what a shame!"
Exclaimed the Sun-
flower, aflame,
"To say such things of me! They *know*
The very opposite is so.

"They know full well that it is *he*—
The *Sun*— who always follows me.
I turn away my head until
I fear my stalk will break; and still
He tags along from morn till night,
Starting as soon as it is light,
And never takes his eyes off me
Until it is too dark to see!
They really ought to be ashamed.
Soon they'll be saying I was named
For him, when well they know 't was he
Who took the name of Sun from me."

The Sunflower paused, with anger dumb.
The Bee said naught, but murmured, "*H'm!*"
'T was very evident that he
Was much impressed — this Bumblebee.
He spread his wings at once and flew
To tell some other bees he knew,
Who, being also much impressed,
Said, "*H'm!*" and flew to tell the rest.

And now if you should chance to see,
In field or grove, a Bumblebee,
And hear him murmur, "*H'm!*" then you
Will know what he's alluding to.

A LOVE STORY.

He was a Wizard's son,
    She an Enchanter's daughter;
He dabbled in Spells for fun,
    Her father some magic had taught her.

They loved — but alas! to agree
    Their parents they could n't persuade.
An Enchanter and Wizard, you see,
    Were natural rivals in trade —
And the market for magic was poor —
    There was scarce enough business for two
So what started rivalry pure
    Into hatred and jealousy grew.

Now the lovers were dreadfully good;
    But when there was really no hope,
After waiting as long as they could,
    What else could they do but elope?
They eloped in a hired coupé;
    And the youth, with what magic he knew —
Made it go fully five miles a day.
    (Such wonders can sorcery do!)

Then the maiden her witcheries plied,
    And enchanted the cabman so much,
When they got to the end of their ride
    Not a cent of his fare would he touch!
Now they're married and live to this day
    In a nice little tower, alone,
For the building of which, by the way,
    Their parents provided the stone.

Then the parents relented? Oh, no!
    They pursued with the fury of brutes,
But arrived just too late for the show,
    Through a leak in their seven-league boots;
And finding their children were wed,
Into such a wild rage they
    were thrown,
They rushed on each other
    instead
    And each turned the
      other to stone.

Then the lovers, since lumber was high,
    And bricks were as then quite unknown,
As soon as their tears were quite dry —
    They quarried their parents for stone.

And now in a nice little tower,
    In Blissfulness tinged with Remorse,
They live like as not to this hour —
    (Unless they have got a divorce).

MORAL.

Crime, Wickedness, Villany, Vice,
    And Sin only misery bring;
If you want to be Happy and Nice,
    Be good and all that sort of thing.

YE KNYGHTE-MARE.

A POST-MORT-D'ARTHURIAN LEGEND.

Ye log burns iow, ye feaste is donne,
    Twelve knyghtes of ye Table Rounde
Slyde down fromme ye benches, one by one,
    And snore upon ye ground.

Ye log to a dimme blue flame has died,
    When ye doore of ye banquet halle
Is opened wide, and in there glyde
    Twelve spectral Hagges ande Talle.

Ye log burns dimme, and eke more dimme,
    Loud groans each knyghtlie gueste,
As ye ghoste of his grandmother, gaunt and grimme,
    Sitts on each knyghte hys cheste.

Ye log in pieces twaine doth falle,
    Ye daye beginnes to breake,
Twelve ghostlie grandmothers glyde from ye hall,
    And ye twelve goode knyghtes awake.

Ande ever whenne Mynce Pye was placed
    On ye table frome thatte daye,
Ye Twelve knyghtes crossed themselves in haste
    Ande looked ye other waye.

METAPHYSICS.

Why and Wherefore set one day
    To hunt for a wild Negation.
They agreed to meet at a cool retreat
    On the Point of Interrogation.

But the night was dark and they missed their mark,
    And, driven well-nigh to distraction,
They lost their ways in a murky maze
Of utter abstruse abstraction.

Then they took a boat and were soon afloat
    On a sea of Speculation,
But the sea grew rough, and their boat, though tough,
    Was split into an Equation.

As they floundered about in the waves of doubt
  Rose a fearful Hypothesis,
Who gibbered with glee as they sank in the sea,
  And the last they saw was this:

On a rock-bound reef of Unbelief
  There sat the wild Negation ;
Then they sank once more and were washed ashore
  At the Point of Interrogation.

The Princess That Wasn't.

IN a very lonely tower,
    So the legend goes to tell,
Pines a Princess in the power
    Of a dreadful Dragon's spell.

There she sits in silent state,
    Always watching — always dumb,
While the Dragon at the gate
    Eats her suitors as they come —

King and Prince of every nation
    Poet, Page, and Troubadour,
Of whatever rank or station —
    Eats them up and waits for more.

Every Knight that hears the legend
  Thinks he'll see what he can do,
Gives his sword a lovely edge, and —
  Like the rest is eaten too!

All of which is very pretty,
  And romantic, too, forsooth;
But, somehow, it seems a pity
  That they shouldn't know the truth.

If they only knew that really
  There is no Princess to gain —
That she's an invention merely
  Of the crafty Dragon's brain.

Once it chanced he'd missed his dinner
  For perhaps a day or two;
Felt that he was getting thinner,
  Wondered what he'd better do.

Then it was that he bethought him
  How in this romantic age
(Reading fairy tales had taught him)
  Rescuing ladies was the rage.

So a lonely tower he rented,
  For a trifling sum per year,
And this thrilling tale invented,
  Which was carried far and near;

Far and near throughout the nations,
  And the Dragon ever since,
Has relied for daily rations,
  On some jolly Knight or Prince.

And while his romantic fiction
  To a chivalrous age appeals,
It 's a very safe prediction:
  He will never want for meals.

The Lion's Tour
A Fable

HIS Majesty the King of Beasts,
Tired of fuss and formal feasts,
Once resolved that he would go
On a tour incognito.
But a suitable disguise
Was not easy to devise;
Kingly natures do not care
Other people's things to wear.

The very thought filled him with shame.
"No, I will simply change my name,"
Said he, "and go just as I am,
And call myself a Woolly Lamb."

And so he did, and as you'll guess,
He had a measure of success.
Disguised in name alone, he yet
Took in 'most every one he met.

The first was Mister Wolf, who said,
"Your Majesty —" "Off with his head!"
The angry monarch roared. "I am,
I'd have you know, a Woolly Lamb."

Then Mistress Lamb, who, being near,
Had heard, addressed him: "Brother dear —"
"Odds cats!" the lion roared. "My word!
Such insolence I never heard!"

His rage was a terrific sight
(It almost spoiled his appetite).
And so it went, until one day
He met Sir Fox, who stopped to say
(Keeping just far enough away,
Yet in a casual, off-hand way,
As if he did n't care a fig),
"Good-morning to you, Thingumjig."

To-day we think it *infra dig*,
To use such words as Thing um jig;
But what is now a vulgar word
In those days never had been heard.
Sir Fox himself invented it
This great emergency to fit.

The King of Beasts, quite unprepared
For this reception, simply stared.

Of course he was not going to show
There was a word he did not know.
He bowed, and with his haughtiest air
Resumed his walk; but everywhere
He went his subjects, small and big,
Took up the cry of Thingumjig.
It followed him where'er he went;
He did n't dare his rage to vent.
Suppose it were a compliment?
His anger then would only show
Here was a word he did not know!
The only course for him 't was clear,
Was to pretend he did not hear.

And this he did until, at length,
Long fasting so impaired his strength
He gave his tour up in despair,
Mid great rejoicing everywhere.

THE FUGITIVE THOUGHT.

WHEN scribbling late one night
I happened to alight
   On the happiest thought I 'd thought
      For many a year.
I hailed it with delight
But ere I 'd time to write
   My pencil had contrived
      To disappear.

Where *could* the thing have gone?
I searched and searched upon
   The table, and beneath it
      And behind it.
I pushed my books about,
Turned my pockets inside out,
   But the more I looked
      The more I could n't find it!

Then I searched and searched again
On the table, but in vain,
   And I fussed and fumed
      And felt about the floor.
And I rose up in my wroth,
And I shook the tablecloth,
   And turned my pockets
      Inside out once more!

"This will not do," I said,
"I *must not* lose my head!"
   So I went and tore the cushions
      From my chair,
Shook all my rugs and mats,
And shoes and coats and hats,
   And crawled beneath the
      Sofa in despair!

Then I said, "I *must* keep cool!"
So I took my two-foot rule
  And I poked among the
    Ashes in the grate.
And I paced my room in rage,
Like a wild beast in a cage,
  In a furious, frightful, frantic,
    Frenzied state!

At last, upon my soul,
I lost my self-control
  And indulged in language
    Quite unfit to hear;
Till out of breath — I gasped
And clutched my head — and grasped
  That pencil calmly resting on
    My ear!

Yes, I found that pencil stub!
But my thought — Aye, there's the rub!
  In vain I try to call it
    Back again.
It has fled beyond recall,
And what is worst of all
  'T will turn up in some
    Other fellow's brain!
So I denounce forthwith
Any future Jones or Smith
  Who thinks *my thought* — a
    Plagiarist of the worst.
I shall know my thought again
When I hear it, and it's plain
  It *must* be mine because
    I thought it first!

THE CUSSED DAMOZEL.

A LOVER sate alone
  All by the Golden Gate,
And made exceedynge moan
  Whiles he hys Love didde wait.

To him One coming prayed
  Why he didde weepe. Said he,
"I weepe me for a maid
  Who cometh notte to mee."

"Alas! I waite likewise
  My Love these many years;
Meseems 't would save our eyes
  If we should pool our tears."

And so they weeped full sore
  A twelvemonth and a daye,
Till they could weepe no more,
  For notte a tear hadde they.

Whenas they came to see
  They could not weepe alway,
Each of hys Faire Ladyee
  'Gan sing a rondelay.

"My Love hath golden hair,"
  Sang one, "and like the wine
The red lips of my Fair."
  The other sang, "So's mine."

"My Love is wondrous wise,"
  Sang one, "and wondrous fine
And wondrous dark her eyes."
  The other sang, "So's mine."

"My Love is wondrous proud,
   And her name is Geraldyne."
"Thou liest!" shrieked aloud
   The other.   "*She is mine!*"

"She plighted ere I died
   Eternal troth to me."
"Good lack," the other cried,
   "E'en so she plighted me!

"Beside my bier she swore
   She would be true to me,
For aye and evermore,
   Unto eternityee."

The twain didde then agree,
   In their most grievous plight,
To fly to earth and see
   The which of them was right.

Alack and well-a-daye!
   A-well-a-daye alack!
Eft soons they flew away,
   Eft sooners flew they back.

For when they had come there
   They were not fain to stay,
To Geraldyne the Faire
   Her silver weddyng daye.

A GAS-LOG REVERIE.

As I sit, inanely staring
  In the Gas-log's lambent flame,
Far away my fancy 's faring
  To a land without a name, —
To the country of Invention,
  Where I roam in ecstasy,
Where all things are mere pretension,
  Nothing what it seems to be.

Folded in a calm serenic,
  On a jute-bank I recline,
Where, mid moss of hue arsenic,
  Millinery flowers entwine.
Cambric blooms — glass-dew beshowered,
  Gay with colors aniline,
Ever eagerly devoured
  By the mild, condensed milch kine.

Now the scene idyllic changes
    From the meadows aniline,
And my faltering fancy ranges
    Down a dismal, deep decline,

Scene of some age past upheaval,
    Where no foot of man has fared,
To a Gas-log grove primeval,
    Where I find me, mute, and scared
Of — I know not — Goblins, Banshees,
    And the ancient Gas-trees toss
Gnarled and flickering giant branches,
    Hoary with asbestos moss.

Now I come to where are waving
    Painted palms, precisely planned,
Rearing trunks of cocoa shaving,
    By electric zephyrs fanned,
Soothing me with sound seraphic
    Till I sink into a swoon,
Dreaming cineomatographic
    Dreams beneath an arc-light moon.

Cupid's Fault

Once Cupid, he
Went on a spree
And made a peck of trouble,
" Ah ha!" cried he,
" Two hearts I see!"
Alack, the rogue saw double.

There was but one ;
What has he done?
How could he be so stupid?
Into one heart
Two arrows dart —
O Cupid, Cupid, Cupid!

In truth 't is sweet
When " two hearts beat
As one" — but what to do
When in one heart
Two arrows smart
And *one heart beats as two?*

ALL ABOARD!

Scene: a railway station.

JUST two minutes more!
O Tempus, stand still,
Stand still, I implore,
One moment, until
I have time to reflect
On what I would say.
Give me time to collect
My senses, I pray,
Until I have said
What my courage was mounting
To say, when instead
I was stupidly counting
The moments that fled!
  O Tempus! you 're flying!
A plague on this parting,
This sighing, goodbying,
This smiling and smarting;
A plague too upon
This — Heavens! it 's starting!
Good bye! —
             There, she 's gone!

KILLING TIME.

The air was full of shouts and cries,
Of shrill "Ha-ha's," and "Ho's," and "Hi's,"
   And every kind of whistle,
And the sky was dark with flying things —
Golf-sticks, balls, engagement-rings,
Novels, rackets, and billiard-cues,
Cameras, fishing-rods, and shoes,
   And every sort of missile.

The ground was black with a seething mass
Of people of every kind and class —
   Matrons, men, and misses,
Ladies and gentlemen, old and new,
Lads and lasses, and children too,
Elderly men with elderly wives —
Hustling and bustling for their lives.
   "I wonder what all this is?"

Said I: "I fear that it may be
Another case for the S. P. C.

'T will bear investigation."
I dropped my book and joined the race,
And struggling into the foremost place,
Behold, the object of the chase
Was an aged man with wrinkled face !
   I was filled with indignation.

His frame was bent and his knees aknock,
His head was bald but for one lock,
   And I cried with anger thrilling,
"This thing must stop; 't is a disgrace
An aged gentleman to chase."
Then everybody laughed in my face.
"This," they cried, " is a different case ;
   It's only ' Time ' we 're killing."

Then it was I observed two things
That grew from his shoulders — two big wings!
   And I joined in the people's laughter.
Tho' killing is often out of place,
A circumstance may alter a case.
So I took my pad and pencil-case,
And for want of a missile, in its place
   I tossed these verses after.

The Mermaid Club.

> *The Mermaid Culture Club request*
> *That you will kindly be*
> *On such and such a day their guest*
> *At something after three.*

I WROTE at once that "I should be
Most charmed," and donn'd my best
Dress diving-suit, — a joy to see, —
And at their club-house 'neath the sea
Arrived at "something after three"
Promptly (unpunctuality
      Is something I detest).
The President, a mermaid fair,
Sat by a coral table,
And read an essay with an air
Intelligent and able
Upon — but you will never guess
The subject — it was nothing less
Than *sunshades* and *umbrellas*.
I really did my very best
To keep from laughing — as their guest.

That it was hard must be confessed
When next the meeting was addressed
On *shoes,* and which would wear the best —
    Tan slippers or *prunellas.*
Then came (it did look like a joke)
Essays on *bonnet, hat,* and *toque:*
Said I, "They must be mocking."
And when at length a mermaid rose,
And read a thesis to expose
The latest novelty in *hose,*
    I felt my reason rocking.
But when at last the thing was o'er,
And I was back again on shore,
    I fell to moralizing.
And as remembrance came to me
Of other clubs *not* in the sea,
Of essays read by ladies fair
Upon the "why" and "whence" and "where,"
    Said I, "It's not surprising."

A SONG.

UPON a time I had a Heart,
    And it was bright and gay;
    And I gave it to a Lady fair
    To have and keep alway.

She soothed it and she smoothed it
And she stabbed it till it bled;
She brightened it and lightened it
And she weighed it down with lead.

She flattered it and battered it
And she filled it full of gall;
Yet had I Twenty Hundred Hearts,
Still should she have them all.

ANGEL'S TOYS.

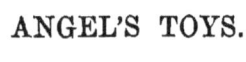

I'VE often wondered — have n't you? —
What all the little angels do
To while eternity away,
When grown-up angels sing and play
Upon their harps with golden strings,
And lutes and violas and things.
What do they do? What do they play
To while eternity away?
After much pondering profound,
Perhaps an answer I have found —
I give it you for what it's worth.
The people now upon this earth,
  Who neither quite deserve to go
  Above hereafter, nor below —
  The prig, the poser, and the crank;
  The snob, who thinks of naught but rank;
  The gossip and the fool — in short,

All nuisances of every sort —
Will change into amusing toys
For little angel girls and boys.
The braggart will confer a boon
By changing to a toy balloon;
The snob tuft-hunter and the bore
To shuttlecock and battledore
Will turn; the highfalutin wights
The angel boys will fly as kites;
The gossip then will cease his prattle,
And be an angel baby's rattle;
The prig — but you have got me there.
Whether in heaven, or elsewhere,
'T is quite impossible to see
What kind of use the prig can be;
By what inscrutable design,
Or by what accident divine,
Or what impenetrable jest
He was evolved, can ne'er be guessed.

THE REFORMED TIGRESS.

A LADY on the lonely shore
   Of a dull watering place
Once met a Tigress weeping sore,
   Tears streaming down her face.

And knowing well that safety lay
   In not betraying fear,
She asked in quite a friendly way,
   "What makes you weep, my dear?"

The Tigress brushed a tear aside;
  "I want a man!" she wailed.
"A man! they're scarce!" the lady cried;
  "I fear the crop has failed!

There is but one in miles, and oh,
  I fear that he is wed!"
The Tigress smiled. "I am, you know,
  A man eater," she said.

"You eat them!" cried the maid, then ceased
  In horror and amaze,
Then sat her down to show the beast
  The error of her ways.

"Men are so scarce," she urged, "I fear
  There aren't enough to go
Around — now is it right, my dear,
  That you should waste them so?

I weep to think of all the men
  You've spoiled ere now," said she.
"And if you eat the rest, why, then
  What will be left for me?"

The hours flew by; she took no rest
   Till twilight, when at last
The contrite beast with sobs confessed
   Repentance for the past.

"Go," said the maid, "take my advice;
   I know what's best for you;
It's cheap and filling at the price;
   Go seek the oyster stew!"

The Tigress lies unto this day
   Upon an oyster bed.
The Lady — so the gossips say —
   Is shortly to be wed.

TWO LADIES.

TO C. D. G. AND A. B. W.

Two ladies, not *real* ladies (no offence —
I don't mean "not real ladies" in *that* sense),
But pictured fancies they — who dwelt between
The pages of a weekly magazine.
Though often in the selfsame week they met,
They were n't exactly in the selfsame set,
And could not know each other. One, I think,
Was done in wash; the other, pen and ink.
The wash lady (again there's no offence —
I use "wash" in its pure artistic sense)
Was a brunette, vivacious, charming wholly;
Neither too slim, nor yet too rolly-poly.

A dazzling smile had this enchanting creature;
Indeed, her most predominating feature
Was a continuous show of glittering pearl;
And on her forehead hung a little curl —
A most distracting little curl; and last,
She had a very slight Hebraic cast.
Gray eyes the other had, serene and clear;
A cold and distant manner; yet I fear
Her looks belied her, for she oft was seen
Lounging about the beach, or 'mid the green,
Of the conservatory's dim retreat,
Always some chappie nestling at her feet.
A first-rate fellow she, and looked her best
When in a golf or walking costume dressed;
In short, the other's opposite in all,
And fearfully and wonderfully tall.
One day, by chance, each occupied a place
On the same page, exactly face to face,
In such a way 't was possible no more
For either one the other to ignore.
Then in an instant burst into a flame
The fire that had been smouldering.
        "How came
You here?" they both exclaimed, as with one
 voice.
(Here I use asterisks, though not from choice

But type has limits, and must play the dunce;
When two young ladies both converse at once.)
* * — ! — * * * ? * * ! ! ! ! ! ! * * * * ! ! * * * ? ? — —
— ! ! * * * * * * * * * ! ! - - - - - ! — — ! - - - - - * * *
* * * — ! ! ! ! ! — — ! — ! — ! !
        I left them to their scenes.
Next day I found the page in *smithereens*,
And I reflected, "It is very sad
That two nice girls should get so awfully mad
About a thing for which, had they but known,
Two artists were responsible alone."

TO THE WOLF AT THE DOOR.

O WOLF, I do not dread thee as of yore,
Time was when I would tremble in my shoes
At sight of thee — when lo! my pity'ng Muse
Brought me wherewith to drive thee from the door.
And since at last, O Wolf, my waning store
Has lured thee back, she will not now refuse
My invocation. So I cannot choose
But cry, "Help! Wolf!" that she may come once more.
Mine is a Muse that listens with disdain
To any call save that of appetite;
And till thou camest all my prayers were vain,
For while my purse was full, my brain was light.
Therefore, O Wolf, I welcome thee again
To speed the Muse — that I may dine to-night.

THE FALL OF J. W. BEANE.

A GHOST STORY.

In all the Eastern hemisphere
You would n't find a knight, a peer,
A viscount, earl or baronet,
A marquis or a duke, nor yet
A prince, or emperor, or king,
Or sultan, czar, or anything
That could in family pride surpass
J. Wentworth Beane of Boston, Mass.
His family tree could far outscale
The bean-stalk in the fairy tale;
And Joseph's coat would pale before
The blazon'd coat-of-arms he bore,
The arms of his old ancestor,
One Godfrey Beane, "who crossed, you know,
About two hundred years ago."
He had it stamped, engraved, embossed,
Without the least regard to cost,
Upon his house, upon his gate,
Upon his table-cloth, his plate,

Upon his knocker, and his mat,
Upon his watch, inside his hat;
On scarf-pin, handkerchief, and screen,
And cards; in short, J. Wentworth Beane
Contrived to have old Godfrey's crest
On everything that he possessed.
And lastly, when he died, his will
Proved to contain a codicil
Directing that a sum be spent
To carve it on his monument.

But if you think this ends the scene
You little know J. Wentworth Beane.
To judge him by the common host
Is reckoning without his ghost.
And it is something that befell
His ghost I chiefly have to tell.

At midnight of the very day
They laid J. Wentworth Beane away,
No sooner had the clock come round
To 12 P. M. than from the ground
Arose a spectre, lank and lean,
With frigid air and haughty mien;
No other than J. Wentworth Beane,
Unchanged in all, except his pride —
If anything, intensified.

He looked about him with that air
Of supercilious despair
That very stuck-up people wear
At some society affair
When no one in their set is there.
Then, after brushing from his sleeves
Some bits of mould and clinging leaves,
And lightly dusting off his shoe,
The iron gate he floated through,
Just looking back the clock to note,
As one who fears to miss a boat.
Ten minutes later found him on
The ghost's Cunarder — "Oregon;"
And ten days later by spook time
He heard the hour of midnight chime
From out the tower of Beanley Hall,
And stood within the grave-yard wall
Beside a stone, moss-grown and green,
On which these simple words were seen:

In Memory

Sir Godfrey Beane.

The while he gazed in thought serene
A little ghost of humble mien,
Unkempt and crooked, bent and spare,
Accosted him with cringing air:

"Most noble sir, 't is plain to see
You are not of the likes of me;
You are a spook of high degree."
"My good man," cried J. Wentworth B.,
"Leave me a little while, I pray,
I 've travelled very far to-day,
And I desire to be alone
With him who sleeps beneath this stone.
I cannot rest till I have seen
My ancestor, Sir Godfrey Beane."

"Your ancestor! How can that be?"
Exclaimed the little ghost, "when he,
Last of his line, was drowned at sea
Two hundred years ago; this stone
Is to his memory alone.
I, and I only, saw his end.
As he, my master and my friend,
Leaned o'er the vessel's side one night
I pushed him — no, it was not right,
I own that I was much to blame;
I donned his clothes, and took the name
Of Beane — I also took his gold,
About five thousand pounds all told;
And so to Boston, Mass., I came
To found a family and name —

I, who in former times had been
Sir Godfrey's — "
    "Wretch, what do you mean!
Sir Godfrey's what?" gasped Wentworth Beane.
"Sir Godfrey's valet!"

      That same night,
When the ghost steamer sailed, you might
Among the passengers have seen
A ghost of very abject mien,
Faded and shrunk, forlorn and frayed,

The shadow of his former shade,
Who registered in steerage class,
J. W. Beane of Boston, Mass.

Now, gentle reader, do not try
To guess the family which I
Disguise as Beane — enough that they
Exist on Beacon Hill to-day,
In sweet enjoyment of their claims —
It is not well to mention names.

www.ingramcontent.com/pod-product-compliance
Lightning Source LLC
Chambersburg PA
CBHW031334160426
43196CB00007B/687